EDGECLIFF

EDGECLIFF

poems by

Angelina Sáenz

FlowerSong Press
Copyright © 2021 by Angelina Sáenz
ISBN: 978-1-953447-63-0
Library of Congress Control Number: 2021950699

Published by FlowerSong Press
in the United States of America.
www.flowersongpress.com

Illustrations and Cover Art by Lorna Alkana
Cover Art Design by Edward Vidaurre
Set in Adobe Garamond Pro

NOTICE: SCHOOLS AND BUSINESSES
FlowerSong Press offers copies of this book at quantity discount with
bulk purchase for educational and business use. For information, please
email the Publisher at info@flowersongpress.com.

For my mentor
Daisaku Ikeda

and

for my parents
Juan Manuel Sáenz y Julieta Padilla

y

para mis muertos

POEMAS

III

En mi está la rebeldía,
encimita de mi carne.
Gloria Anzaldúa

Second Shift

Canvas-bag teacher-mom, I sigh through front door
Sons kick off shoes and toss backpacks
Flop on sectional and fall asleep

I start fireplace

Hostile MFA class in two hours
Manuscript spilling out of backpack reminds me

Change into stretchy pants and faded Obama t-shirt
Lady and Cocoa skid around me
Pinch up their shit and wipe up their piss

Review homework folders
Preheat oven to 375
Decide on chicken broth or milk
to soften sixteen frozen mash potato medallions

Feet up
Eat other half of leftover carne asada burrito

Outside
dense slate storm clouds

gather

We are off to a most excellent start!

If You Want a Divorce
the First Thing We're Going to Do Is Sell This House

You and I
Early thirties
No savings
Fico hell

Oak beams and stained glass
Skylights and double-hung windows
French doors and Andalucían cork oak trees
seduce us into battle
to buy this home

Both of us
Long brown hair
Standing on porch
Me in a paisley green blouse
You in a Cal State Long Beach tank top
White bandana around your head
Golden key to front door unseen in your palm
Birds of paradise frame photograph

Only ones
in our family
to own in Los Angeles

Siblings moved east or south
Bought low and laughed that we bought high

On his way out after helping us move in
brother laughs

> "I hope your things are still here
> when you come back tomorrow"

Barrio amnesia

Soon cross threshold
with newborns in bundles of blankets

You'd turn on soft lights with baby's cry
Bring me water
Lay next to me
hand on your forehead
as I nursed into night after dark night

After twenty-two summers

winter

If you're happy and you know it...

Humidity transports me

       to musty brick homes along dusty roads
       moist sunrise rooster calls
       ragged dogs roaming on roofs

       to Tepic, Nayarit

Neighbors in my Tia's living room tiendita call

       ¡Quiero!

I turn in stinky sheets dried on rainy clothes line

Muffled kitchen voices and clinging of dishes
Chancla shuffles on concrete floor and fan's soft whir
ease me into waking hours

Uncle paces in and out of floral curtain doorway
judging my lazy yanqui-ass for still being in bed
at 6am

Sidewalk broom bristles to dark men
in thin button-up shirts and sooty slacks
Cracked feet in worn huaraches and calloused hands
load up triciclos de carga
Elote helados tamales frutas flores

Unforgiving tropical sun angrily shines
on walk along uneven cobble-stone street

Human mass on bus radiates moisture
The deaf and mute guitarist
who has memorized death climbs
up rusty stairs plays random strings and screams
from the top of his lungs into my hot ears

Helado de limón nos refresca en la sombra de los guayabos en la plaza central

Nos subimos a un taxi
ventanas medias abiertas
nubladas por la humedad

Humedad

      Parallel dimension

And I'm not talking about damp
I'm not talking about

      Seattle
      San Sebastián
      San Francisco

 I'm talking about tropical humidity

      When it is not humid
      my feet are on the ground
      I am working mothering writing hustling

      But this morning I am waterside in Miami

      The mist crawls across the ocean

as humidity wraps my heart in banana leaves

Practicing...

Little Man

Shaking your hips in my classroom mirror
Your Fedora hat to the side
You find a feather in my craft box
Tuck it in

> *How do I look mama?*

> *You look sharp mijo*

> *I'm leaving then*

I watch you
walk down the hallway with a lean
to your first-grade classroom

So… there are a couple of things about this picture. First, my dad's and stepmom's house is a treasure chest. They are experts at finding, buying and reselling (at a much higher price) used things. So when we go, we always come home with treasures they're giving us. I got a fabulous new office chair yesterday. But I DIDNT realize that Ayende took four sunglasses and guess which ones he loves? Aye is a total fashionista ya'll.

Big Boy

From jump
you were the brick
then the cinder block

                                    now you're the wall

25 pounds at 3 months
Dr. Fleiss said

       Only give this baby your milk
       until further notice

At 9 months Abuelita said

       ¿Sólo le has dado tu leche?
               Sí
       Hoy le vamos a dar de comer y beber

She prepared worn plastic sippy cup with water
Tenderly peeled frijoles de la olla

Tu estabas encantado

In preschool
your teachers swore you were naughty

Your two-year-old body would run
to hug your buddies
and you'd knock them the fuck down
They'd bawl their eyes out

Psychologist called in to evaluate you
She told them you were beautiful
and to stop fucking confiscating
the Thomas the Train you kept in your pocket

Thick chose you
Inhabits your broad shoulders

Thank you T-shirt shop on Figueroa and York
that sells Dickie's husky size
The only pants that fit you

When you met Grandpa
when I reunited with him
after twenty-three years
you said

> *Mama, I look like Grandpa*
> *That's where I get my body from*

Location: Yank Sing
Duuuuuuuude!

Mom's Refuge

I thought
being a shit-show
followed you to the afterlife

So I didn't think you could help me
with my insomnia
the night before
my first day of MFA classes

And then I sensed you saying

> *Mija, who I was on earth*
> *is not my eternal identity*
> *Here, I am powerful*
> *Here, I am composed*
> *Here, I am complete*
> *Here, I am healed*
> *And the least I can do*
> *from the other side*
> *is caress your forehead tonight*
>
> *Sleep, corazón*

Cosas.

First Day of MFA

Professor and I
only ones above thirty

Photographer says
      Faculty ID for you?
               No
               I'm a student here

Mental note
      Old white man professor
      assigns old white men to read

Classmates know references to shit I don't
      Fuck you Shakespeare
      and fuck me for having never read The Tempest

Someone asks
      What's the word for people who don't like other people en masse

I say
      Sociopath

they all look at me

Another student says

      Misanthrope

they all nod

LMFAO

Discuss Jack Spicer's letters to Lorca

I ask

> *Did Lorca really say that?*

Pause

> *This is a fictitious exchange between Spicer and Lorca, Angelina
> Lorca had been dead for 30 years when this was written*

I'm an asshole
Someone made a mistake in accepting me into this program

Things I do during our zoom faculty meeting!

Tinder

Te invito a mi casa
Llegas
All 6 feet and swimmer shoulders of you

En tus brazos
el sofá se convierte en nido

Platicamos de El Salvador
bosques sin sentido en Virginia
swim team at Marshall High
Buddhism and the Lotus Sutra
        Our history

Turnamos leyendo versos de Benedetti

Your full strong mouth finds mine
Warm gentle hands contour thighs waist back

        Before we go too far
I whisper
        Lo dejamos aquí, tengo que trabajar mañana

You stand up
Gran caballero que eres
Mt. Everest at your crotch
        y nos despedimos

Amanezco a una mañana lluviosa
Me envías un poema que me escribiste

Pienso
        Este hombre

Singing from the top of my lungs while I cook breakfast!!!
Que viva mi querida raza...

Shit-show Wednesday

Monday
Just a few feet
from Nordstrom Rack entrance
Calvin Klein white pantsuit in
XX size
How unusual
It's a sign
We will win

Tuesday
It's wear-a-white-fucking-pantsuit-day bitches

Colleagues say
> *Are you getting married at lunchtime?*
> *and*
> *I look like hell in white, otherwise I would have joined you*

Election results party
my house
Festive spirals to confused panic
Flurry of text messages begins

> Leave guests
> to walk dogs
> Usually loud and busy street
> deserted
> Television glows light the sidewalk
> Impossible
> mocks my heart

Decide to sleep with the boys
Son asks in the dark
> *Can he really be president, mama?*

I pull him in closer
Their sleeping breath holds vigil

Wednesday
3am
Screenshot headline
Pigs freeze and hell flies

Get up
Recite chapters 2 and 16 of the
Lotus Sutra
Toast waffles
Fold burritos
Throw in load of laundry
Print 24 narrative reports
10 parent conferences ahead of me
First one
7am

> Parent and I cry for five minutes
> Then discuss five year-old's progress

Teaching partner says

> *It's an art day today*
> *Color outside the lines*

Parent in hallway
at Day of Dead display
Turns to me with swollen red eyes
We embrace

School is shelter
I'm taking in the wounded

Get home at 5pm
Boys are with their dad
Crawl into bed
Sleep until tomorrow

Thursday
Level 5 hurricane of
information

Some are stunned
The smartasses knew

I'm at dog park by 2pm
Autumn sun warms me
People all around me

I am alone

Friday
Who to blame
racist white folks
white women
third-party voters
non-voters
neo-liberals
democratic party
the media
intellectuals
the elite
russia
red states
blue states
canada
voting laws
electoral college
hillary
donald
the Bern
karma
neglect
misogynists
the disconnect
mark zuckerberg

our unwillingness

to see

and know

Saturday
The same elder
who called
during Katrina
and said

> *New Orleans*
> *is the bottom*
> *of a slave ship*
> *right now*

Calls again

> *Who votes*
> *for a man*
> *that supports waterboarding?*
>
> *Look*
> *did they miss the kindergarten lesson?*
>
> *You don't vote for a bully*
> *not for student government*
> *and not for the President of the United*
> *States*

Phone on speaker
while I cook fish sticks and mac n'cheese

Boys wait for me
to binge watch

Stranger Things

Sunday
Constipated since Wednesday
morning

I finally
take a shit

Bagels, coffee and mama's first Monday on summer break!

Why didn't Leo Come with You?

Because we're getting a divorce

Really? Since when, mija?

Since six months ago

Why didn't you tell me?

I didn't want to upset you

Why would I be upset?

I didn't want you to worry about me

I never worry about you cabrona
You're made of steel

So what are you going to do now?

I'm going to read and write

Read and write, huh?
That sounds about right
And that doesn't surprise me

Sábado en obra.

Hello Professor

33

I read Hugh Selwyn Mauberley
and I didn't know what the hell the poems were about

Seriously
I read it twice
And then
I sat at my table
and thought for a long time
about what to do

I looked up Pound in the American Poetry Foundation
Read about his life
His significant contribution to modern poetry
Who he was associated with
Who he influenced
What Hugh Selwyn Mauberley meant for him

For some reason though
I feel like researching him
makes me a cheater
I don't know how I would understand otherwise

Anyway
Just wanted to share
I did all of this other reading
so that I could understand
the actual reading

I hope that is ok

Teaching break...

I'm downstairs

35

Open door for you
Trail me
Hand reaches up my skirt
Caresses my ass

In the kitchen
Our favorite place to fuck
Green tea steam
curls around my fingers
I look down at mug

You lean against the refrigerator
and watch me

    How did it go?

You avoid my question
Reach for me
Your heavy lips take my shoulder

Me hundo

Limp
I curl into you
Traffic outside lulls me to sleep
Moon crosses the sky
You turn me over

    Quiero más

Mi vida loca...

Mija

I told you

>   When it gets heavy
>   When the grown people around you
>   are out of their fucking minds
>   Desiring to absolutely annihilate one other

I told you

>   to say to yourself

>>   *I will create a different life for myself*
>>   *I will create a different life for myself*

Because saying that is what got me through
the madness of my childhood

I want to override your turmoil

>   Your feeling that

>>   it's better

>>>   to be dead

than alive

That was too much to ask of you
because one day
after middle school
you went home
and

My mom and dad. 1970

II

Anyone who has ever struggled with poverty
knows how extremely expensive it is to be poor.
James Baldwin

963 Edgecliff Drive

Single-mothers-on-welfare oasis

30 apartments organized around
zigzagging staircases where we played tag
leafy patio corners where we put on puppet shows
bridges leading to solitary landings and pebble gardens
Mediterranean ambiance in the middle of the city

Josie screaming

> *Don a-run on my rampas*

Vowing to tell our mothers we were being bad

Sparkling swimming pool overlooking Bellevue Park
was the childcare for an army of latchkey kids

Within five years
cement was poured
into every corner
that mattered to us

They started with the planters
then moved to the gardens
and last was the pool

Concrete landscape
sealed our destiny
of death and loss to come

Palmas.

Mom

at the stove
hand on hip
flipping corn tortillas
with bare fingers
on flame

She'd fling them
flying saucer style
to our hungry mouths
gathered around plates
of white rice and beans

I waited for the day
when my fingertips
could touch the flame, too

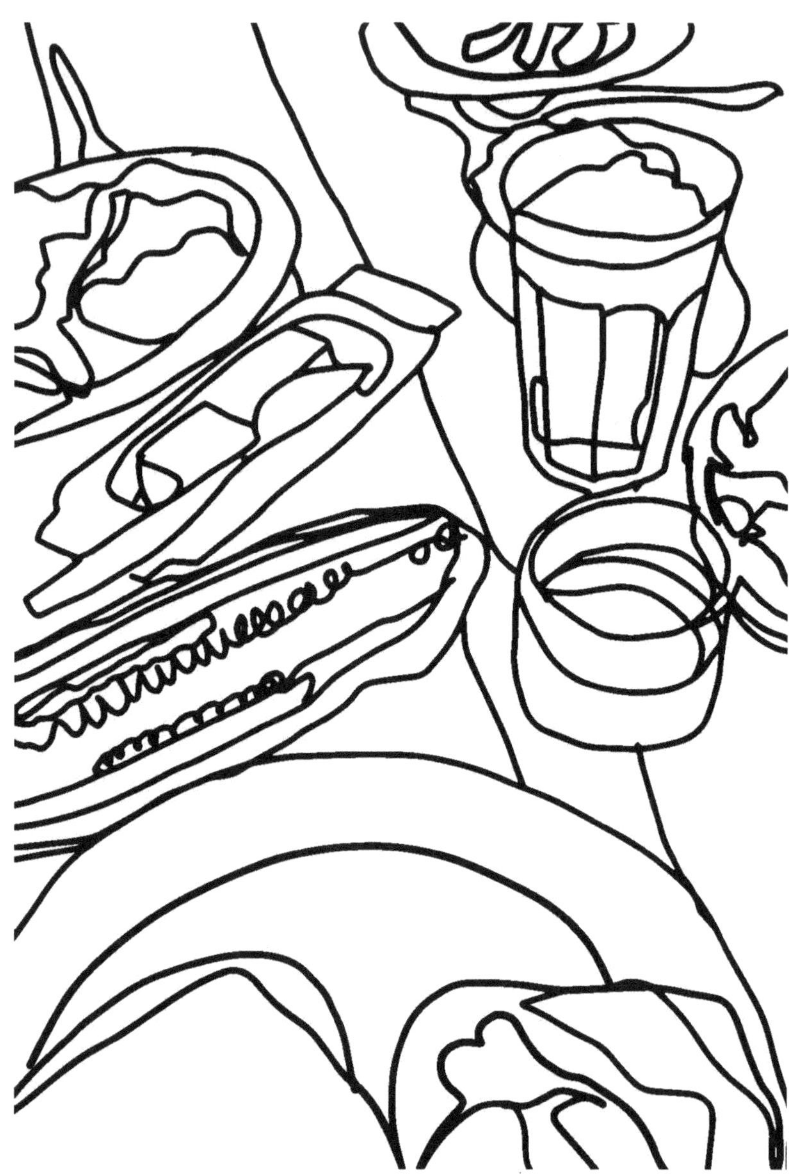

Eugene Oregon
En casa de Darin y Adam. Me recuerda que si queremos, cada momento puede ser un momento cósmico. Gracias Pamela por presentarnos.

"We are travelers on a cosmic journey, stardust, swirling and dancing in the eddies and whirlpools of infinity. Life is eternal. We have stopped for a moment to encounter each other, to meet, to love, to share. This is a precious moment. It is a little parenthesis in eternity."
— Paulo Coelho, *The Alchemist*

Norma in Pink Sweats

I stand at the plate glass window
on the corner of Sunset & Maltman
watch bubbles bounce in deep fryer
as pale donut dough turns golden

You and trays of glistening glaze wave us in

As big as a trailer home
Soft freckled face framed by long brown hair
always pulled tight into a pony tail
You didn't fit between the counter and the wall
so, you'd shuffle sideways to take our order

> *Have some milk*
> *Don't drink a suicide before school*
> *And don't put pop rocks in your drink*
> *you'll choke*

Gripping the counter with one hand
Scooping up ice with the other and
punching our cup into every flavor of soda
You'd serve it to us
with a chocolate twist or maple bar

Green leather ledger kept
our little names in perfect penmanship
and under our names
the amount of everything we consumed

On the 14th and the last day of the month
You'd give us a paper for our mother
that showed what we owed

She always paid

My tío and I, 1975, Tepic, Nayarit. And I had a cast because I put my hand through the clothes wringer on the washing machine...

Gina

sold Hello Kitty products
at 7:30am
every school morning
from her living room
on Micheltorena Street

Inebriating smell of Hello Kitty plastic
lured me into the display of
purses, pencil bags, erasers, tin boxes and note pads

You can take whatever you'd like and pay me later

I did

and also learned
how to steal from my mom
and begin a life of debt

"Mama, can I use the book you wrote about me for my reading log?"
Why did I get sentimental right now when my son finds it perfectly
normal to write my name as the author and to find his family's story
in a book? Oh my god!!!

Roaches Weren't No Thing

They fell out of cabinet doors
Crawled across Saturday cartoons

We flicked them
shook them
stomped on them
put out RAID bombs

                                   I was unaffected

But the day we decided
to throw away our corroded couch
and lifted it to find a country of them
including a whole family of albino roaches

                                   I was finally
                                   disgusted

Guerrilla Family Apartment 16

Stay-at-home mom and a father who provided for his family
They'd pass our front door
with armloads of groceries

    There go the fucking gorillas, Mom would call out

as they heaved up the steps

    Yeah fuck those slobs, we'd respond

from kitchen table where we were playing monopoly

In the parking lot
their brand new 1982 burgundy Monte Carlo
mocked our sickly green 1975 Ford Pinto

Their footsteps
would trigger mom into a rage
of banging the next 100 dents into our ceiling with loyal broomstick

Every time the Department of Child and Family Services
showed up to ask

      do you have enough to eat
      are you ever alone
      does your mother hit you
      is there anything you'd like to tell me

                  yes
                  no
                  no
                  no

Mom swore it was the Guerrillas who had called
and she vowed to make their life miserable

They lived above us for seven years
endured the endless horror
that boomed from our home

Drop

Suspend body in air on one hand
Freestyle
Anyone can step in

Bitch-ass calls me out
Battle consumes me
Rhythm grinds

> *Just start to chase your dreams*
> *Up out your seats, make your body sway*
> *Socialize, get down, let your soul lead the way*

Beat twitches away drunk mother waiting for me
Swing daily hunger into a back-spin
JR's blood on Cadillac white leather
after getting jumped in his front seat last night
Clapped and shouted away by crowd

> *Shake it now, go ladies, it's a livin' dream*
> *Love, life, live*
> *Come play the game, our world is free*
> *Do what you want but scream*

Snap harder
Pound chest in and out
Shuffle in Chinatown slippers bought on Broadway
starched black kung-fu suits
Midcity Knights embroidered on the back
Loosens with each lock

> *The DJ plays your favorite blasts*
> *Takes you back to the past, music's magic, poof*

My mom and dad. Taking pictures of each other next to his new
Pinto. Come on! Hollywood, 1972 (she's pregnant with me in this pic)

The Year I Turned Five

Oh-ho, I need you by me, to guide me,
to guide me, to hold me, to scold me,
'Cause when I'm bad I'm so, so bad

Dark apartment
Mom's Donna Summer party
In dining room
Mom's Hindu friend
White polyester suit
Black button-up shirt
Volcano of thick black hair
Collar turned up
Pulls me into him
One finger to his mouth

as in

                Quiet

Other hand in my underwear
Then fingers
up my vagina

I stand there

You On Our Dirty-Ass Couch

glass of water and your mumu dress
gathered between your legs
Comb and a shitload of rollers off to the side

Front door wide open
as Don Cornelius serenades introduction of the S.O.S. Band

> *You know you ought to slow down*
> *You been working too hard*
> *And that's a fact*
> *Sit back and relax awhile*

You part sections of your hair with precision
no mirror
Dip your comb into the water
Bring up a whole section like a tidal wave
Bring the whole thing down
snug against your scalp

> *Take some time to laugh and smile*
> *Lay your heavy load down*
> *So we can stop and kick back*
> *It seems we never take the time to do*
> *All the things we want to, yeah*

Neighbors come in and out with their coffee mugs
You shake the comb high in the air
finger-popping between your task
until your whole head is covered
in pink sponges

Maybe it was

the roaches
that crawled across
TV screen

or the soiled laundry
or sink piled high
with crusty dishes

the sheets thrown over
the holes in the doors
that you punched through

the graffiti walls
everyone tagged on
when they kicked it in our bedroom

or maybe it was the night
when mom took a bat
and bashed in your record player
and LPs and smashed
your Def Leppard mirror
and tore all of your heavy metal posters
off the wall

that you decided
to meticulously build and furnish
a cardboard clubhouse
in the field across the street

You dragged rugs and cushions
turned on candles and we'd huddle
with the other kids on those scary nights
Caterpillars and pincher bugs
often joining us

My name is

one hand high in the air
snapping

> *Der-ek*
> *So-ri-a-no*

other hand on your hip
daisy duke shorts
pink muscle shirt
cropped curly wet hair
bobby socks
and your white reeboks

> *Happy Egg Day girl!*

I'm in a yellow romper and pig tails
I'm holding my pillow sack
of stolen Easter eggs and candy
from the Bellevue Park Hills

I'm looking at you

and the light coming from behind you
in the doorway
makes you glow
like a saint

My beautiful mother, died 27 years ago today, when I was 20. She was 41. Here she is, at the Taco Bell, on Western, nearly Beverly, in 1969. Fresh out of foster care, she's holding my older brother in her arms. As the years pass, I feel her presence stronger and stronger in my life, gaining momentum in understanding how hearts and this existence works, she is fiercely by my side, protecting and guiding me, from my own arrogance and foolishness that can so easily hijack my destiny. ¡Julieta Padilla, presente!

Dark Night

11pm
Your drunk friends
show up at the house

Where's my mom

They can't tell me

Speed walk through Bellevue Park
toward Jade Garden restaurant

You must be
between the park
and Droopy's house

I find you
face down on the sidewalk
Passed out

Sit next to you
Wait for you to

wake up

How to eat a Free-Lunch Bologna Sandwich

1. Get your box
2. Carefully arrange all of the contents in front of you
3. Bite off the corner of the mustard
4. Bite off the corner of the mayonnaise
5. Smash spread it on the bread
   (cuz mofos don't provide any utensils)
6. Take a bite
7. Let it stick to the roof of your mouth for a bit
8. Swallow

The way to start the day...

I'm calling Tia Pola in Tepic

was like saying

    Scatter, bitches!

because we'd run and hide
and then you'd find our asses
one by one
and make us talk to her

    for like five minutes

        in our broken-ass Spanish

Hiiiiiiiiiiiii!
Friday.

Glass House

The morning my mother showed up
with an ogre's lump on her forehead
two purple bloated eyes
stitches on her cheek
lips that looked like two blisters about to pop

and her dead stare

I thought a beast had taken over her body

Drunk driving
police pulled her over
at the 4th street exit of the 110 northbound

Belligerent
she refused to get out

They beat her out
boot baton fist
then locked her up
in Sybil Brand

A witness in the front seat
they took my sister to foster care

returned her to us a week later

mute

Jan Hendrix Landfall Exhibit

2am, Wednesday, July 29, 1981

Front door open to cool dawn
Neighbors appear with matrimonial offerings
Mom provides the coffee

It is Princess Diana's wedding

Brown black white single
food-stamp-mothers riveted
as Diana waves from glass carriage
Veiled stoic chiseled jaw and blonde feathered hair framed

They hold their breath
as Diana's 25-foot-long wedding gown train
is dreamily arranged at the mouth of Westminster Abbey

Camera zooms into terrified radiance

She is only a few years younger than all of them
but they talk about her
as if she were their daughter

Sweeping camera shots
of central London
Themes
Tower Bridge

None of the women in my living room
will ever know these places

But I will

Inevitable pulling out of photos. My mom. Mexican passport.
6-years-old, maybe? #chula #shemademe

The day

you got to the bottom
of the hill at Lucile and Marcia
and didn't brake

crashing straight into
Rod and Helen's living room

My soul left my body
again

One DUI under your belt already
attending AA meetings twice a month

your drunk-ass convinced them
not to call the cops

Claim it as a hit and run

And those nice liberal white folks
who always took us
to No War in Central America marches
who kept us off the streets by inviting us to work
at their tiny theater on Melrose and Heliotrope
paying us in dinners eaten in their living room
that opened up to the most beautiful wild garden
helped you out that day

For the next few months
every time I passed by the construction
I hated you

The northeast corner

of Bellevue Park
Wooded hillside
of three-story pines

Offering me low-lying branches
I'd take off my shoes and bare-footed
I'd step and reach for sappy branch after sappy branch

Emerging to sway in its crown

Hollywood stretched out before me

I was 12 he was 15

He told me I was a real woman
Told me to keep it a secret

He'd find excuses
to take me away from family dinners
and make out with me in the parking lot

My pubescent body wanted him
but I didn't tell him it was ok
the day he unzipped his pants
while he was eating me out
and shoved himself inside me
strap of my training bra falling off my shoulder
as he finished

I'm sitting on the toilet
blood in the water
I can hear Mom come in the front door
Asking where everyone is
He says I'm in the bathroom and he's waiting for my brother

When I come out
He is on the couch watching TV
Mom tells me
to come to the kitchen
and help her
cook
the guys

dinner

Don't break or scratch those cabrona

Sitting on the filthy rug
Touching your vinyl for the first time

Harold Melvin and the Blue Notes
Mary Wells & Teddy Pendergrass
The Shirelles & The Manhattans

> *If you don't know me by now*
> *Well I've got two lovers*
> *It's my party and I'll cry if I want to*
> *Looks like another love TKO*
> *This is dedicated to the one I love*
> *Dry your eyes, there is no need to cry*
> *Sad girl, you look so sad, did he break your heart*

Memorizing the lyrics
to the soundtrack
of our lives

How To Get Your Shit Out of the House
When You've been Evicted

74

1. Don't fuck with the padlock
2. Time yourself fifteen minutes
3. Break the puto window
4. Grab a laundry basket, bags and pillow cases
5. Fill it with clothes and important papers
6. Leave the rest of your life behind
7. You'll never see it again

III

Escribí. Escribí poemas de amor y canciones
desesperadas. Me deprimí tanto que hubo días
en que no podía salir de la cama. Me atrevo a
decir, sin embargo, que esa crisis marcó el final
de un círculo completo de mi vida y que al
hacerme tocar fondo me hizo también emerger
con un conocimiento de mí misma que quizás no
habría podido obtener de otra forma.
Gioconda Belli

Your precious hands

always need to be busy

Hot wheels cars
and elaborate race tracks as a toddler
turned into four hours of daily, sophisticated
origami folding in the 2nd grade

So the first time you saw
a video of someone handling a butterfly knife
you were captivated
Convincing me to buy you a plastic replica
you practiced spinning snapping twisting

The rule was
do not take it out of my house
The first thing you did was
take it to school
and then we were in the dean's office
and they just kept saying

It is illegal to bring
a weapon
or the replica of a weapon
onto campus

The consequences are
expulsion and arrest
expulsion and arrest
expulsion and arrest

What these motherfuckers didn't know
is that you were on track
to expel your damn self out of that school

You had already taken the SAT
at the age of 12
scoring above the national high school average

They didn't know
that the doctor who administered your IQ test
said you were the youngest person
to score at genius
in just an hour

They didn't know that a year and half later
you would be admitted to Cal State LA
skipping middle school and high school entirely
at the age of 14 and get a 3.2 your first semester
having taken 18 units

They didn't know
They never know
They just see brown children
and all they can think is

expulsion and arrest
expulsion and arrest
expulsion and arrest

My dad gave us 20 granadas AND taught the boys how to get all the
seeds out. Does anyone want any? We have so much!

Huichol at Burke Williams

Face down on massage table
Breathing in all my new millennium decisions
Este lujo
So far from the dirt floor of a remote ranch
in the Nayarit jungle that you knew as home

Turn over in the dim light
and see a vision
of your dark brown face
at eight years-old
matted black hair, tussled on top
rugged braids hanging to the side
thick lips and fierce eyes
hover over me

And then
gone

Massage therapist asks me to take a deep breath in
I do
and then I breathe out
wondering
why you appeared to me

     Como te extraño, mamá

I've been on vacation for a week and sending off pics to parents after sleeping for a week. This particular picture captures everything. Brings tears to my eyes. Happy first day of summer y'all. We've lived to see another summer.

Hello

Voice I love
floats to me
from front door

Dazzling smile appears in the doorway
You look at me
as you take off your shoes
Put your wallet on the dresser
Take off your watch and silence your phone

Jump into bed and inhale deeply at my neck

You smell so good

Arms and legs wrap around me as you hold me tight

Let me take a quick shower

Damp body comes out with towel wrapped around your bulge

Jump into bed and fingers search for my opening
I exhale as your mouth swallows my breast

Climb on top of me
and plunge deep
Your head pressed against mine
I say

I love you

You grip me tighter and say

I've missed you so much

Wiggle your hips and hold yourself deep inside

> *Que rico*
> *Que sabroso, Angelina*

My pussy is in your mouth
I moan

Back on your knees
Pull both of my legs straight up and cross them at the ankles
Lift my hips into you and you watch yourself in the mirror

Then you fall
our chests cave in and out
in rhythm

Rendidos

Condo

The day I told you
I was selling my house and moving into a condo
you cried

> *We don't give up our land mija!*
> *This is all my fault!*
> *I don't want the boys living in an apartment!*
> *Is it your debt?!*

In my usual nonchalant manner
that drives you fucking crazy
I answer

> *Dad it's a condo. It's not an apartment.*

You ignore me
begin migrant labor camp story

> *Mija there's rape, murder, knives, blood, abuse.*
> *You don't know what I've seen*
> *cuando la gente se encima...*

You plead

> *No apartment building*
> *You need a house*
> *space and walls to keep everyone away*

I rock in the recliner
ocean breeze and chimes fill the silence

> *It's a fucking condo Dad. Not a migrant labor camp.*

Dear professors (All of you Fuckers)

Thank you
for your email
stating how disappointed you are in me
and your workshop notes about how
you don't see poetry
in my poetry

I wrote you back requesting a meeting
and in that meeting I explained

    I'm a single mom
    I've never studied literature
    I have homeless family members living with me
    That I do all my writing between 4am and 6am when my children are asleep
    That I teach kindergarten all day and then commute two hours to you
        That my son is suicidal
        That I am broke
        That I am a first-generation college student
        That I have to talk myself out of dropping out everyday
        That my toxic family dynamics still affect my life
        That I've had kidney infections and my hair is falling out
            since starting this program
        That you add to my trauma
            when you non-chalantly talk shit
            about my work
                which is the story of my people
                of my mother
                of my ancestors
                of the kids that I grew up with
                who ended up murdered, in prison or on drugs
                of my perpetual grief

and that whatever the fuck I give you
is an offering of my life and sacrifice

You just look at me
from across the table
with your stupid stare
and say

How would I know all that?

Oh my god... 1987. Hollywood.

Most of the Women I Know

Were molested by the time they were in 5th grade

None of the men strangers
All of them
neighbors, fathers, uncles, brothers, cousins, friends

Where the fuck were our mothers?

> They knew and blamed us
> Or didn't know and still blamed us
> Or they didn't know
> > and said it happened to them too
> > so get over it
> > or
> > what the fuck were we doing there anyway?

Not one mujer has told me
that their mother stood up for them
and confronted or banished perpetrators

True and sad story

Events are always the same
Quick snatch in a crowded or empty room

> Wounding shame that follows
> decimates

Scar tissue tightens and stretches
through motherhood, our careers, our relationships

Look at us
grown-ass women in our forties
coffee mugs in our hands
at our kitchen table

crying
about the time

                                    that man
                                    touched us

91

Researching and revising.

I Come from a Place Where All We Knew Was to Be Ghetto Fabulous and Together

Before you start
taking out
your pinche black and white fotos
of your tatarabuelo de Francia
con sus ojos verdes
and your bisabuela Eugenia
from the Tarahumara tribe
know
I don't have a single goddamn picture
to show you
of my ancestors

Before you pull out your map
showing me
where fulano boarded his boat in the Bay of Biscay
arriving in your mother's hometown in Zacatecas
or the pueblo
that four generations of your gente
were born into
know
that my mother was born in the Nayarit jungle
to my fourteen-year-old grandmother
and no one can say who the father is
and that I may not even be a Padilla
porque mi bisabuela era puta
and there is no judgement there

Before you tell me
of caps and gowns
cheerleaders and jocks
and that you were voted
most likely to succeed
know

I come from a place of flunking fools
0.0 grade point averages

Before you share your tips
about the bands playing in Echo Park
or the best ramen in Silverlake
or how Hollywood is now called the Eastside
know
my muertos' blood pooled on your corners
as men masturbated in their cars on Sunset
and my mother
lay facedown
intoxicated
on the Lucile midnight sidewalk

Andando...

None of the New Guys Matter to Me

I can take them or leave them

I don't feel the fire when I touch them
When I look into their eyes, it's just sex, not love
I don't look at their bodies like I gazed at yours

      when I'd stop at the foot of the bed and say

          Let me look at you

You'd rub your cock up and down
Eyes locked

I don't run my hands along the curves of their bodies
Grasp their asses as they thrust into me
They don't whisper

          Que rico
          Que sabroso

I don't give them my life like I gave you my life
They don't have my heart like you still have my fucking heart

We'd roll on our backs
and you'd wipe me down and wipe yourself down
Reach for me and I'd curve into you
We'd talk for hours and then do it again

          Nunca lo he negado Angelina
          Tu, para mi, eres especial y única

Maybe you're at home writing me a poem too
or maybe
*yo aquí escribiéndote y tu allá borrándote

Tonight I miss you
I've come far enough to know
that we cannot resuscitate the corpse of our love

But I'm thinking
of how you used to hold me
in the dark

*Jaime Sabines poem

Aug 14, 2021 A baby with a baby. All sleep-deprived and shit.

Boys

Thank you
for being
champions

Thank you for pushing through
the heartache of Dada's and my divorce
only to face nights alone
cooking for yourselves
and putting yourselves to sleep
while I was going to school at night
to learn about and write poetry

We missed each other
I was always working on my thesis
and you just wanted me
to watch movies with you
or play a board game

You would say

> *Mama, don't burn the food*

>> as I hunched over a book
>> or my computer

or

> *Mama, did you start dinner
> or are you writing a poem?*

The day I turned in my thesis
I asked Dada if you all could stay home from school
and drive with me to school
and we took pictures of us all holding the manuscript
and putting it in the box together

With only five dollars
I drove to the donut store
and we bought two milks and chocolate bars
and then drove to the hill
where you can see planes land at LAX
and you drank your milk and ate your donuts
and I cried
and you said

    Mama, what does it take to make such heavy things

fly

Being a mother... so glad I get to do it in this lifetime. "A woman who takes this efficacious medicine will be surrounded and protected by these four great bodhisattvas at all times. When she rises to her feet, so too will the bodhisattvas, and when she walks along the road, they will also do the same. She and they will be as inseparable as a body and it's shadow, as fish and water, as a voice and it's echo, or as the moon and it's light.
"On Offering Prayers to the Mandala of the Mystic Law - Nichiren Daishonon c1200

Yo soy

la generación
entre

mi mamá
sentada sobre la tierra
lodosa y fértil
comiendo elote
en la selva de Nayarit

y

mis hijos
sentados en escaleras de piedra
desgastados por los siglos
comiendo gelato de limón
en la plaza mayor de Segovia

Teotihuacán, 2016

Your Beauty and Your Goodness

for Leo

Can't see the computer screen
to begin typing my ode
to your beauty and grace

Because the tears of appreciation
for the luminous human being
that you are, won't stop falling

I've had the honor to love you
and create children with you
for 22 years

Your heart of gold
The purity of your love and devotion
will harvest you a lifetime of joy and fulfillment

I'm on a plane writing this
I don't want anyone to see my crying
I don't want strangers to hear my crying
So I'll stop for now

I am so deeply indebted to you
And I'm sorry that we are separating

The only way to not feel this pain
is to not do this at all but I have to go now
I really do
My soul wants to be on its own

I know you understand
And you've told me
not to apologize anymore

So I'll stop

We start our new journeys
Our 22 years are not in vain

Let's make the rest of our lives
a tribute to the greatness
we've lived thus far

I love you

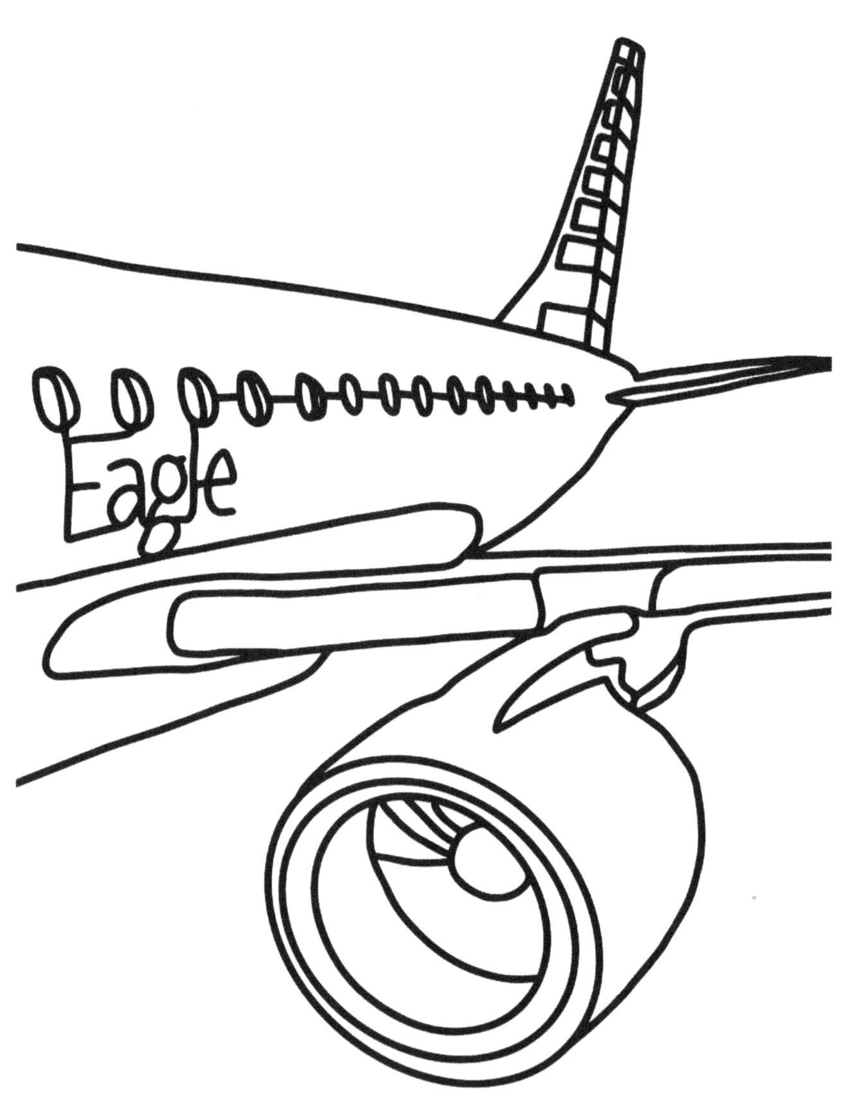

Some Chicanas walk on to the tarmac at LAX to catch little airplanes to fly the fuck out of Trumpland! Bye!

Revising a Poem About Us

You were the love of my life
I hope you are well

        I will never forget
        our time together

Dear professors

I am the poem

Acknowledgements

Thank you to my sons, Amir Terrazas and Ayende Terrazas, for your sincere hearts, wisdom, love and devotion. Son mi esperanza para un mundo mejor.

Thank you to the editors of the periodicals in which these poems first appeared: "I Come From a Place Where All We Knew Was to be Ghetto Fabulous and Together," in *Every Other*, "How to Get your Shit Out of the House when You've Been Evicted," *COCKPIT Voice Recorder: Paris* "Yo soy," *COCKPIT Voice Recorder: Paris*, "Humidity Transports Me" *Acentos Review*.

Big props to the amazing illustrator Lorna Alkana, my dearest friend who has been drawing my life since 2017. When I thought of the cover, I thought of you, and of course, you came through.

Thank you to Faye Peitzman and the late Jane Hancock and the UCLA Writing Project; Willie Perdomo and our workshop crew of the VONA/ Voices Workshop for Writers of Color; Sandra Cisneros, Sherwin Bitsui, and our workshop crew of the Macondo Writer's Workshop; and special thanks to my MFA workshop classmates; all of you gave me the space, the encouragement, and the confidence I needed to believe in and continue to develop this manuscript.

Thank you to Edward Vidaurre and FlowerSong Press for bringing it to the fucking world with our voices and for publishing my first librito.

Thank you to Guy Bennett, my MFA advisor whom none of these poems are about, for asking me after I graduated if he could continue to call me to inquire about finishing this manuscript, and for calling every few months through the years to ask how it was going.

Thank you to my favorite poetry mafioso, Matt Sedillo, who also asked if he could keep calling me about finishing and submitting my manuscript, and who did keep calling and asking, and who finally set some random-ass deadline, and kept calling me leading up to the deadline, causing me to actually finish this mofo. If you wouldn't have given me that deadline homey, this shit wouldn't have happened. Gracias, mil.

Special thanks to my Buddhist organization, SGI-USA, for teaching me how to use my Buddhist practice to believe in the dignity of my own life and to take responsibility for everything, changing all poison into medicine. Nam Myoho Renge Kyo.

My acknowledgements page was originally two pages long, because I have all of you, my family and friends to thank, for all of your encouragement and support for me and my writing, since forever. I know you. I see you. I am indebted to you. And we will continue to celebrate a lifetime of telling our stories, hecho y derecho, con honestidad, humor, dolor y curiosidad. c/s

About the Author

Angelina Sáenz, M. Ed, MFA is an award-winning public-school teacher and poet whose work focuses on memory, mujeres and motherhood. She is a UCLA Writing Project fellow, an alumna of the VONA/Voices Workshop for Writers of Color and a Macondo Writer's Workshop Fellow. Her poetry has appeared in venues such as *Diálogo*, *Split this Rock*, *Out of Anonymity*, *Angels Flight Literary West*, *Every Other*, *Cockpit Revue Paris* and *The Acentos Review*. She is the host of the monthly poetry reading La Palabra at Avenue 50 Studio in Northeast Los Angeles.

Every poem in *Edgecliff* feels like a short film of Angelina Sáenz's memory that you can taste, smell, and feel in your bones. You will dance to the rhythm of the words. You will cry. You will laugh. You will be transported. And at the end, feel honored that she shared her world with us.

— **Megan Tan**, Podcast Host and Producer

Even while humidity wraps Angelina Sáenz's "heart in banana leaves," she is brimming with laughter, compassion and gratitude in poems that celebrate her sons and catalog her own coming of age as a mother, educator and Buddhist. Recalling the episodes that made her the strong woman she is, the stanzas in *Edgecliff* show her finding refuge in her second shift and receiving timeless wisdom channeled from her ancestors. These poems meditate on her daily journeys but end up revealing something much more extraordinary. I was inspired by her resilience and reminded by her realness that progress is incremental but when you stay with it, the results are incredible. Angelina Sáenz is for the people.

— **Mike Sonksen**, author of *I Am Alive in Los Angeles*

Angelina Sáenz' work is the poetry that must—poetry born of sinew and struggle, born of the necessary hard exterior shell and the heat of the still burning heart within. Sáenz' voice is unrelentingly honest and spare—powerfully in possession of itself. She writes, "You add to my trauma/when you non-chalantly talk shit/about my work/which is the story of my people/ of my mother/of my ancestors/of the kids that I grew up with/who ended up murdered, in prison or on drugs/of my perpetual grief," and that same tough and tender voice demands and owns its space in our literature and our hearts, "whatever the fuck I give to you/is an offering of my life and sacrifice.

— **ire'ne lara silva**, author of *furia*, *Blood Sugar Canto*,
CUICACALLI/House of Song, and *FirstPoems*

In *Edgecliff*, Angelina Sáenz's poems are honest, raw, and unrelenting. Her poems are polaroid snapshots of memories, from a girl's childhood as chaotic as a hurricane to a dauntless single mother who "creates a different life for herself" and her sons con ánimo y corazon.

— **liz gonzález**, author of *Dancing in the
Santa Ana Winds* (Los Nietos Press)

Angelina's Sáenz's poetry opens pathways to her most personal life experiences withher stunningly bold and intimate poems. Sáenz walks you down her neighborhood's dark and dangerous streets in search of a loved one whom she finds face down on a street corner. In another poem, she encourages her students to "color outside the lines" on art day. You might tear up after learning that it's all true. There are gifts here. Some are not easily unwrapped.

> — **Ron Baca** is a poet and lifelong resident of L.A.'s Eastside and is a volunteer tutor at Homeboy Industries

Edgecliff is the song one woman sings as she peers out over the new world she is fashioning for herself. And as she steps into that world, she pays homage to everything that brought her to this place, here, where she can finally breathe. In her unique, clear-eyed style, Angelina Sáenz examines poverty and violation, love and determination, cruelty and stupidity, motherhood and the triumph of birthing oneself against the odds. *Edgecliff* is a grit chronicle, rhythmic and very much like song. Quiero más.

> — **Donna Spruijt-Metz**, author of the chapbook *Slippery Surfaces*

Angelina Sáenz's stunning *Edgecliff* takes us to places needing to be seen. Each powerful hit-you-in-the-gut word sounds and rhythms uncover the resilience, the power, the luminosity of a people who are Los Angeles. Sáenz sends us on a journey of familia with past and present histories of loss, blood, shame, and survival. James Baldwin wrote, "nothing can be changed until it is faced." Sáenz is presenting us the opportunity to look, and to look intently.

> — **Amelia María de la Luz Montes**, Americanist (Chicanx/Latinx) LGBTQ scholar

Sáenz allows us to truly enter a world where "a beast" takes over a mother's body. In this collection her poems do not flinch in the face of truth. *Edgecliff* occasionally breaks from the power of Sáenz's truncated rhythm to offer comic relief, where we are instructed to "3. Break the puto window" and "6. Leave the rest of your life behind"—and for just a moment we do.

> — **Cynthia Guardado**, author of *Endeavor*

Sáenz's voice in *Edgecliff* is fearless, familiar, refreshingly free of affectation, and marked by a fierceness that holds our immediate attention with intimate stories about poverty, alcoholism, sexual abuse, and single motherhood. Stripped of unnecessary adornment in crystal-clear lyric moments, we are allowed to enter a sacred memory-space where a girl finds joy amid poverty and heartbreak in "pebble gardens" next to "zigzagging staircases," stepping barefoot on low-lying branches of three-story pines at the northeast corner of Bellevue Park, the woman in pink sweats that always fed her a meal on the corner of Sunset and Maltman, and remembering the mother glowing in a doorway—and not the mother "face down on the sidewalk / passed out" or turned away from men's violent acts upon her daughter. "I'm looking at you and the light coming from behind you makes you glow like a saint," Sáenz writes. *Edgecliff* tells us a story of survival out of the snapshots in a woman's photo album; together, Sáenz's poems blaze with the beauty and power of telling the truth.

— **Leslie Contreras Schwartz**, 2021 Academy of American Poets Laureate Fellow and the 2019-2021 Houston Poet Laureate, author of *Black Dove / Paloma Negra*

Edgecliff is a banquet of poems shaped in absolute honesty, feeding us the right amount of chisme, heartache and triumph all working together to keep self-love and survival at the forefront.

— **Karla Cordero**, author of *How To Pull Apart The Earth*

Trust. That is what the debut poetry collection *Edgecliff* is asking from us as its readers. Each poem invites and trusts us with its vulnerability, lessons, narratives, and hardships. We live in apartments, get evicted from apartments, listen in on conversations between fathers and daughters, fight with our mothers, watch relationships dissolve and emerge all on the same page. Sáenz's work trusts us to relive our own childhood memories, but this time with amor and meditation.

— **Luivette Resto**, author of *Unfinished Portrait* and *Ascension*